Those were the days ...™

British & European Trucks of the 1980s

VELOCE

Also from Veloce –

Those Were The Days ... Series

Alpine Trials & Rallies 1910-1973 (Pfundner)
American 'Independent' Automakers – AMC to Willys 1945 to 1960 (Mort)
American Station Wagons – The Golden Era 1950-1975 (Mort)
American Trucks of the 1950s (Mort)
American Trucks of the 1960s (Mort)
American Woodies 1928-1953 (Mort)
Anglo-American Cars from the 1930s to the 1970s (Mort)
Austerity Motoring (Bobbitt)
Austins, The last real (Peck)
Brighton National Speed Trials (Gardiner)
British and European Trucks of the 1970s (Peck)
British Drag Racing – The early years (Pettitt)
British Lorries of the 1950s (Bobbitt)
British Lorries of the 1960s (Bobbitt)
British Touring Car Racing (Collins)
British Police Cars (Walker)
British Woodies (Peck)
Café Racer Phenomenon, The (Walker)
Drag Bike Racing in Britain – From the mid '60s to the mid '80s (Lee)
Dune Buggy Phenomenon, The (Hale)
Dune Buggy Phenomenon Volume 2, The (Hale)
Endurance Racing at Silverstone in the 1970s & 1980s (Parker)
Hot Rod & Stock Car Racing in Britain in the 1980s (Neil)
MG's Abingdon Factory (Moylan)
Motor Racing at Brands Hatch in the Seventies (Parker)
Motor Racing at Brands Hatch in the Eighties (Parker)
Motor Racing at Crystal Palace (Collins)
Motor Racing at Goodwood in the Sixties (Gardiner)
Motor Racing at Nassau in the 1950s & 1960s (O'Neil)
Motor Racing at Oulton Park in the 1960s (McFadyen)
Motor Racing at Oulton Park in the 1970s (McFadyen)
Motor Racing at Thruxton in the 1970s (Grant-Braham)
Motor Racing at Thruxton in the 1980s (Grant-Braham)
Superprix – The Story of Birmingham Motor Race (Page & Collins)
Three Wheelers (Bobbitt)

Truckmakers series

DAF Trucks since 1949 (Peck)

www.veloce.co.uk

First published in August 2013 by Veloce Publishing Limited, Veloce House, Parkway Farm Business Park, Middle Farm Way, Poundbury, Dorchester, Dorset, DT1 3AR, England.
Fax 01305 250479/e-mail info@veloce.co.uk/web www.veloce.co.uk or www.velocebooks.com.

ISBN: 978-1-845844-17-2 UPC: 6-36847-04417-6

British Library Cataloguing in Publication Data – A catalogue record for this book is available from the British Library.
Typesetting, design and page make-up all by Veloce Publishing Ltd on Apple Mac. Printed in India by Replika Press.

Contents

Foreword & Acknowledgements

Foreword

While the 1970s had been a decade of dramatic change within both the British and Continental European trucking industries, few could have predicted that by the end of the decade only 44 of the more than 60 mainstream manufacturers that had originally rolled into the 1970s would still be in business.

British truck manufacturers had been the hardest hit, with just 11 out of the 18 firms in business at the start of the 1970s still in the truck building business in 1980. AEC, Albion, Guy, and Thornycroft had all fallen victim to the merciless British Leyland axe, and Scammell didn't have long to go before it was also for the chop. Commer had gone and the Dodge brand was on its last legs, whilst Dublin-based Dennison would be history within 12 months of the new decade.

Despite much hoo-ha during the 1970s about increased gross vehicle weights potentially bringing Britain closer to harmonisation with European trucking legislation, it was not until the government white paper of 1982 – setting out plans for 34 tonnes on four axles, 38 tonnes on five axles, and 44 tonnes on six axles – that truck manufacturers and operators had something firm to work with.

So, whilst trucking firms evaluated how equipment designed for higher gross weights would benefit both their operational capabilities and profit margins, many truck manufacturers took a long hard look at the spiralling costs of developing and building new models in the face of tough and ever increasing competition.

Seddon-Atkinson was already in foreign ownership, and Foden was acquired in 1980 by US truck manufacturing giant Paccar. Across the Channel, Barreiros, Berliet, Bussing, Henschell, and Saviem had been already been swallowed up by major brands, whilst Fiat, Magirus-Deutz, OM, and Unic had morphed into Iveco, and the 1980s witnessed something of a feeding frenzy as specialist builders and major firms were snapped up by rivals. Just 35 mainstream European truck manufacturers survived into 1980, compared with 44 in 1970, and the 1980s would see amalgamations and acquisitions on a major scale, reducing the total even further.

As a result of the increase in gross vehicle weights, manufacturers entered into something of a power race, with multi-cylinder turbocharged and intercooled diesels of 300 and even 400hp becoming ever popular. The decade also witnessed the decline of proprietary diesels as truck builders which installed such power plants as Cummins, Detroit Diesel, Deutz, Gardner, Perkins, and Rolls-Royce were swallowed up by rivals keen to offer only their in-house engines.

In just over 20 years, Britain and its Continental neighbours had gone from largely isolated and parochial truck markets to something akin to a free-for-all, with most manufacturers needing to enter a neighbouring market to survive. It was against this overly-competitive market that Bedford pulled the plug altogether on truck production, and Ford threw its lot in with Iveco. However, this is only half of the story, and you'll need to read about each manufacturer listed to understand the big picture.

This book focuses exclusively on trucks built by manufacturers based in Britain and Europe, wherever they may have been used. However, it does not attempt to be the definitive guide to the decade, nor does it attempt to be a concise catalogue of every make and model produced. With some 46 different manufacturers to squeeze in, the references can be no more than a snapshot.

Acknowledgements

I would like to dedicate this book to the large number of people, literally from around the world, including truck manufacturers, dealers, drivers, journalists and enthusiasts without whose help this book would not have been possible.

Many people who worked in the trucking industry during the 1980s have fond memories of those days, and this book is a tribute to a decade of amazing change and a vast array of manufacturers, the likes of which we'll never see again.

It won't be possible to mention everybody who has had a part in making this book possible, but I will try to list as many as I can: Gyles Carpenter, Max Chern, Dennis Childs, Clive Davis, George B, Andrea Dal Porto, Dave Gibson, Mike Glendinning, David Gothard, Juraj Hlavac, Arthur Ingram, Niels Jansen, Mervyn Jones, Trevor Jones, Lex Meeder, Rik Meeder, Martin Perry, Jonathan Pye, Bill Reid, Len Rogers, Rod Simmonds, Richard Stanier, and Rick Todd.

Colin Peck
Wraysbury, England

British manufacturers

Bedford

The Bedford trucks division of Vauxhall Motors was one of the UK's most well-respected and long-established manufacturers of light and middleweight trucks.

The long-standing TK, which had been introduced in 1960, had often been criticised for not having a tilt cab, and by the time the model was finally dropped in the late 1980s, it had become completely outdated. The successor to the TK, the tilt-cab TL range, was introduced in 1980 and, curiously, was produced alongside the TK for a number of years, but never proved as popular as its predecessor.

Bedford had entered the 1980s with a large product range of both civilian and military trucks, and had taken the plunge and entered the heavy end of the truck market in 1974 with the introduction of the Detroit diesel-powered TM range. However, the two-stroke V6 and V8 DD engines did not find favour amongst British hauliers, who were not used to the high-revving

Left: A Bedford TK operating at 35 tonnes GVW? This New Zealand TK had been modified locally with a Cummins VT903 V8 diesel, cranking out 295hp for some seriously heavyweight work. (Courtesy Rod Simmons)

Despite being launched in the 1960s the long-standing Bedford TK remained in production until the late 1980s.

The Bedford TL was introduced in 1980 as a successor to the TK but never proved as popular.

characteristics of the two-stroke diesels, and although the Cummins E290 had been a limited option since the late '70s, it was only when both the E290 and the L10-250 became more generally available in 1982, that operators found the TM more acceptable.

Whilst Bedford struggled to upgrade its light and medium weight models and work towards making its heavyweight models more operator-friendly, a crushing blow was delivered when Bedford failed to win the UK Ministry of Defence contract for 4x4 four tonne trucks, despite having a long history of supplying such vehicles

The V6-powered TM was never the hit that Bedford had hoped it would be. (Courtesy Dave Gothard)

Two-stroke Detroit Diesel V6s and V8s did not find favour with British hauliers, and although a Cummins option proved more acceptable it was too little, too late for Bedford. (Courtesy Clive Davis)

to the MOD. The devastating loss of the military vehicle deal to rival Leyland, which was seen by many observers as being politically motivated, didn't go unnoticed by Bedford's parent, General Motors, in Detroit, and this loss together with fiercer competition from European truck manufacturers saw Bedford withdraw completely from truck manufacturing in 1986.

Following the demise of Bedford truck production, the manufacturing facility in Dunstable was sold in 1987 to AWD Ltd, a company owned by David John Bowes Brown who ran a construction machinery company as well as building all-wheel-drive off-highway trucks. The Bedford name was not part of the deal, so the AWD name was used on highway trucks for the UK market, whilst the AWD-Bedford was allowed for export market trucks.

Despite the new company's best efforts, which included winning some sizeable export orders, tough trading conditions saw the new venture cease after just over four years, finally bringing an end to one of Britain's most famous truck marques.

Dennis

Best known as a manufacturer of fire appliances, buses, and refuse collection vehicles, the Guildford-based firm tried, unsuccessfully, to expand its range of general haulage trucks throughout the 1960s, and even went as far as offering a lightweight 32 tonner.

However, its haulage trucks were not overly popular, and sales were sparse. Following financial difficulties, the company was acquired in 1972 by the Hestair Group and renamed Hestair Dennis. The company re-focused on new fire engine technology, and building trucks export.

As a result the company finally recovered from huge losses and ventured back into the bus market. Heartened by its export successes, Dennis commissioned a modified version of the Delta-2 chassis and re-entered the UK domestic truck market in 1978.

The 16-ton GV Delta 16.18 was launched in 1980 for tipper and haulage use with a choice of five wheelbases. The standard power unit was the ubiquitous Perkins T6.354, rated at 155bhp, and while Dennis had hoped to sell 100 Delta chassis during the first full year of production, the recession put paid to that with sales dipping below half that number.

Some of the most unusual Dennis trucks of the period were five outside broadcast vehicles for the BBC. Built initially as 6x2s with a plated gross vehicle weight of 22 tonnes, at least one ended up as an 8x2. This Dennis 'eight-wheeler' had a Perkins TV8-540 (215bhp) engine driving via an Allison automatic transmission.

By the mid 1980s Dennis was focussing almost exclusively on municipal vehicles and buses, and so made the surprise announcement that the company was to end its long association with Guildford. As a result, 500 jobs initially went at Guildford, when all municipal vehicle manufacture was transferred to a new Dennis Eagle plant at Warwick. At the same time, Dennis cab production was switched to the recently acquired Hestair Duple plant at Blackpool.

For a while the original Guildford site produced bus and coach chassis and fire appliance chassis in two separate workshops. However, the company was sold to Trinity Holdings (formed from a management buyout from Hestair Group) in 1989.

Dennison

Dublin-based Dennison ventured into truck production in 1975, following the sale of its trailer business to Crane Fruehauf. Despite a positive start, it barely managed to build 250 trucks and tractors before production ceased in March 1981.

George Dennison comments, "We were buying all

Apart from fire trucks and refuse collection vehicles, Dennis produced some unusual Perkins V8-powered outside broadcast units for the BBC.

of our parts, including the cab, in sterling, and when Ireland joined the EMS in March 1979 we lost 25 per cent of our buying power literally overnight. Whereas our competitors, such as Volvo and Scania, etc, by being on the Continent, didn't lose out at all.

"Also, the second oil crisis kicked in, and Maggie Thatcher came to power, and the general economy in Ireland and the UK went into decline. We ceased truck production in March 1981, just as the five years were up, and we went back to building trailers. However, closing the truck business proved very costly and it cost us 1.3 million Irish punts to close it up."

Dodge

Following Chrysler Europe's collapse in 1977, and the sale of its assets to Peugeot, the Chrysler/Dodge British and Spanish factories were quickly passed on to Renault Véhicules Industriels, and the French company gradually re-branded the range of vans and trucks as Renaults through the 1980s.

The last British-built 500 K-series, designed originally around the noisy Cummins Vale V6 and V8 diesels, were built in 1980, although the former Commer Commando, which latterly became the Dodge 100 series, was marketed for a while by its new owners as

The old Commer Commando had already morphed into the Dodge 100 series when the brand was acquired by Renault. This unusual 6x2 with sleeper cab conversion is seen here in New Zealand. (Courtesy Trevor Jones)

the Renault 100 and was sold in some markets as the Renault Commando until being deleted in 1987.

ERF

ERF entered the 1980s as Britain's last truly independent truck builder, but with the country in the midst of a recession it wasn't long before the bottom had fallen out of the truck market. ERF put its fire engineering division up for sale, and in 1982 launched the C-series, an updated version of the trend-setting B-series previously launched in 1974.

The E-series (there was no D-series due to the use of that letter by rival Ford) was launched in April 1986, using a more refined version of the glass fibre cab, and it was a huge success for the company. It was also around this time that ERF fell out of love with Gardner diesels, which had been offered in its chassis since the very first trucks were built.

Gardner, which had fiercely resisted turbocharging, finally launched its first all-metric engine, the 15.5-litre 6LYT, in the mid-1980s, but with a price tag some £20,000 more than a comparable Cummins or Perkins (Rolls-Royce Eagle) diesel, it was to prove a sales disaster. So, when Gardner launched the 310bhp turbocharged 6LXDT in 1988, both ERF and Seddon-Atkinson revealed they had no plans to offer the Gardner engine as an option.

A year later ERF cemented its relationship with Cummins by launching its most powerful E-series yet, the E14-365.

Foden

Foden entered the 1980s in poor health. It had a new range of trucks, but was struggling to sell them. It had launched the Fleetmaster and Haulmaster models, developed from the Universal in 1977, and both

Two-axle tractor units were still popular in the mid 1980s as they could operate at 38 tonnes GVW with a tri-axle trailer. (Courtesy Clive Davis)

The ERF C-series was launched in 1982 as an updated version of the B-series. (Courtesy Len Rogers)

The ERF E-series was launched in 1986 and for the first time in the firm's history there was no Gardner diesel option. (Courtesy Martin Perry)

featured versions of the stylish Motor Panels S90 steel tilt cab.

A year later Foden introduced a new GRP version, dubbed the S10, which was outwardly similar to the steel Motor Panels cab but some 75 per cent lighter.

The company had bounced between profit and loss during the late 1970s, and by 1979 was faced with redundancies and short time working due to large losses. It won a short respite early in May 1980 with a multi-million pound order from the Ministry of Defence, but this was not enough to facilitate long-term recovery and, with stocks of unsold trucks mounting, it was forced to cut its workforce.

When the receivers were finally called in, a deal was brokered with Paccar, the leading North American truck manufacturing conglomerate, and the future of the Sandbach-based manufacturer looked assured. Paccar was determined not to compromise Foden's reputation for quality, but still had to embark on draconian cost-cutting and redundancy measures to get the ailing firm back on its feet.

Paccar also set about using its US experience in building both Peterbilt and Kenworth trucks to design a new range of lighter Fodens, and by 1983 the use of aluminium chassis components and wheels had become an option.

Curiously, Foden struck up an alliance with rival Ford in 1982, when production of the Ford Transcontinental was transferred from Ford's Amsterdam plant to Sandbach to take advantage of some spare manufacturing capacity at the plant. Production of the big Ford ended in December 1983, when Ford discontinued the Transconti in favour of a new 38 tonne GTW 6x2 Cargo.

Around the same time Foden introduced a Caterpillar engine option – the first time Cat engines had been

The Foden S10 Haulmaster eight wheeler was launched in 1978 and had engine options up to 320hp. This example has a more modest 201bhp Gardner 6LXCT turbo.

The revised Foden S10 appeared in 1983 and had cleaner lines than its predecessor. (Courtesy Martin Perry)

A significant addition to Foden's 1980s line-up was the S106T 6x4 tractor unit, taking inspiration from parent Paccar's north American truck expertise. (Courtesy Martin Perry)

offered in a UK-built truck – and this was another step towards the company's goal of building every single truck to specific customer order. In 1987 Foden launched the re-styled 4000 that set the scene for the next decade.

Ford

The long-running medium weight D-series finally gave way to the Ford Cargo in 1981, which featured a stylish new cab with side windows that extended down to cab floor-level, assisting the driver with parking in urban areas.

The heavyweight Transcontinental range was discontinued in 1984, and replaced with a heavyweight range Cargo tractor with units ranging from 28-38 tonnes GVW; the heaviest powered by the 250bhp Cummins L10.

In 1986, Ford sold its European truck operations to the Italian Iveco Group, and subsequent trucks were badged as Iveco Ford.

Ford D1000? Although the Ford D-series was discontinued in 1981 it didn't stop this New Zealand tipper operator adding an axle or two, a trailer and probably a 290hp Cummins VT903 V8 to operate at 35 tonnes+ GVW. (Courtesy Rod Simmons)

Leyland

Following the nationalisation of the British Leyland Motor Corporation (BLMC) by the British Government in 1975 to help save the UK's largest motor manufacturer from dire financial troubles, the truck division was renamed Leyland Vehicles, which subsequently became Leyland Trucks in 1981.

The division had already dispensed with AEC, Albion and Guy during the 1970s, and with Scammell in decline, the main focus was on the core Leyland brand.

The Ford Cargo was altogether a more purposeful-looking truck than its predecessor. (Courtesy Clive David)

Ford replaced the H-series Transcontinental in 1984 with Cargos capable of operating at up to 38 tonnes GVW.

With production of the stop-gap Leyland Marathon transferred to the Scammell plant at Watford – to take up some of the spare capacity resulting from phasing out of the Crusader – Leyland was able to focus on completely new models.

The result was the stunning T45 Roadtrain, launched in 1980. Viewed by many in the industry as the truck that Leyland should have launched five years earlier, it was perhaps too little too late, as by then the UK truck market was already swamped with high-quality competitors, and Leyland's attempts at marketing the truck in Europe amounted to little success. Available initially with the AEC-based TL12, Cummins and Rolls-Royce Eagle diesels, most operators favoured the RR option and the old TL12 was discontinued in short order.

Leyland introduced the obscure Landmaster in the 1980s primarily for export markets.

The Roadtrain cab was designed from the outset as a modular unit so that it could be adapted in size and scale to fit other models within the Leyland portfolio – such as the Roadrunner, which was launched in 1984 to compete against the popular Ford Cargo in the above 7.5 tonne sector.

Leyland has forged a long-standing relationship with DAF in Holland – going back to the supplying of 680 series engines back in the 1950s – so it was only natural that when Leyland was struggling to survive in the mid '80s, it would hold talks with the Dutch truck maker to discuss a merger. As a result a new organisation known as Leyland-DAF was formed in April 1987 when the Dutch truck maker took a 60 per cent controlling interest in the ailing British firm. It is estimated that at the time of

Leyland introduced the Roadtrain in 1980 to positive market reviews, but it was the truck that Leyland should have built five years earlier. (Courtesy Clive Davis)

the merger DAF had just eight per cent of the UK truck market, whilst Leyland had some 17 per cent.

Within six months DAF had opened a brand new UK headquarters and, at its launch party, unveiled the brand new Leyland-DAF 95 series featuring the Cabtec tilt cab, designed in conjunction with ENASA in Spain. The new truck featured the DAF 11.6-litre ATI engines, developing 306, 352 or 383bhp, depending on specification, and were light years ahead of the Leyland Marathon, being produced just ten years earlier.

The Roadtrain was only available initially with the 290hp TL12 engine. It was some time before Cummins options became available. (Courtesy Clive Davis)

Following the merger of DAF and Leyland, the 95 series quickly put the Roadtrain in the shadows. (Courtesy DAF Trucks)

Scammell

Scammell's reputation and ability to develop specialist trucks was probably the main reason that its Watford plant survived the fate that had befallen most other Leyland group truck brands during the 1970s. Despite the phasing out of the Crusader range in 1981, just 13 years after it had been introduced, Scammell was entrusted by Leyland to develop and build a range of new trucks designed for the 1980s.

The first of the new trucks was the Leyland Landtrain, a heavyweight bonneted truck aimed at the export market. Scammell was able to use the same cab and bonnet for its own replacement for heavy haulage Contractor – dubbed the S24. These new trucks were available in both rigid and tractor versions, with 6x4 and 6x6 options up to a gross train weight of 200 tonnes.

Cnt'd page 26

Scammell entered the 1980s more a builder of specialist Leyland vehicles than a firm forging its own destiny. The first new truck to roll out of the Watford works was the replacement for the ageing Scammell Contractor, now dubbed the S24 Leyland Landtrain.

Following the development of the new Constructor 8, Scammell used the Roadtrain cab to build heavyweight 6x4 trucks, which were simply known as the S26. (Courtesy Gyles Carpenter)

The Scammell S26 proved a major export success for Leyland. (Courtesy Mervyn Jones)

Scammell's reputation in the construction industry was held in esteem by Leyland, so the Watford plant was also entrusted with the production of the new Leyland 8x4 rigid, known as the Constructor 8. Scammell used the same modern tilt cab on a range of premium 4x2, 6x2 and 6x4 tractors, known as the S26 range, which effectively replaced the Crusader range.

A military S26 6x6 version with Rolls-Royce 350 power was produced, and this was later offered in 8x6 form to the British Army in 1986 for the hooklift-equipped DROPS vehicle requirement. A year later Scammell learnt that its tender for 1522 8x6s had been successful, but as DAF had acquired the Leyland group, the S26s would now be built at the Leyland plant, and the Watford plant would be closed.

Sadly, the Tolpits Lane plant closed a year later, and the Scammell name was consigned to the history books. However, the S24 and Nubian ranges, together with rights to the Crusader and Commander, were acquired by Unipower, which opened a new production plant in West Watford.

Seddon-Atkinson

By the 1980s Seddon-Atkinson was already a well-established marque in Britain, having been formed some ten years earlier when Atkinson was acquired by rival Seddon and the two brands subsequently merged into one new truck range.

In 1974 the firm was acquired by the American giant International Harvester, and a year later the

The kiss of death for Scammell. Despite winning a 1500+ vehicle contract from the British army for S26 8x6 rigids, the acquisition of parent Leyland by DAF saw production switched to Leyland, and Scammell's Watford plant bulldozed flat.

last Atkinson-badged truck rolled down the assembly line. That same year saw the launch of the innovative Seddon-Atkinson 400 series, which set new standards in UK truck design and captured 20 per cent of the UK truck market within its first 12 months of production.

The face-lifted 401 series was launched in 1980. (Courtesy Clive Davis)

This superb Rolls-Royce Eagle-powered 401 highlights the style that made the Seddon-Atkinson a top seller. (Courtesy Rick Todd)

The faced-lifted 401 range was launched in 1981. The firm's involvement in the bus and coach industry ended in 1983, when production of the Pennine 7 chassis ceased, and at the same time the company was acquired by Spanish automotive group ENASA, thus becoming a subsidiary of Pegaso.

The Seddon-Atkinson Strato appeared in 1988 and featured the Cabtec cab shared with Pegaso and DAF. (Courtesy Bill Reid)

The Strato appeared in 1988, replacing the 411 series, and used the Cabtec consortium designed cab; shared jointly with DAF and Pegaso.

Unipower

With a background in third axle conversions, 4x4 timber haulage tractors, and even sports cars, Unipower relocated to Thames Ditton in Surrey in 1977, following its purchase by AC Cars. So it was quite an unusual, if not a bold move, when Universal Power Drives acquired the remnants of Scammell in 1988 when the Leyland group's new owners, DAF, decided to discontinue production of Scammell trucks.

Whilst Unipower set out to provide continuity support for worldwide operators of Scammell trucks, the firm also acquired the manufacturing rights to the Scammell Contractor and Crusader.

Originally designed as a tank transporter, the 750hp Unipower 8x8 proved to be a very capable heavy haulage tractor. (Courtesy Gyles Carpenter)

European manufacturers

Astra

Like many European truck manufacturers founded in the aftermath of World War II, Azienda Sarda Trasformazione Autoveicoli started in Italy in 1946 as the Astra workshop, refurbishing former military vehicles and adapting them for civilian use.

The firm had been using Fiat drivetrains and components virtually since its inception, so it was no surprise when it was acquired by Iveco in 1986.

The half cab Astra proved popular in the Italian construction industry. (Courtesy Andrea Dal Porto)

This 440hp Astra 6x4 is seen at work on Malta. (Courtesy Jonathan Pye)

Barreiros / Dodge

After the Chrysler Corporations took control of Spanish trucker maker Barreiros in 1969, so began a policy of re-branding some of the trucks with the Dodge logo. Those sold in the UK received the Dodge badge, whilst the company continued constructing trucks under the name Barreiros in Spain until 1978, when they were all branded as Dodge. That same year, Chrysler Europe was acquired by Peugeot. The company and factory was passed over to Renault in 1981, and the truck range was re-badged once again.

The former Barreiros-Dodge range was re-branded Renault following its acquisition in 1981. (Courtesy Rik Meeder)

Turkish-built BMC Fatih trucks were produced under licence from Leyland. (Courtesy Rik Meeder)

This Yavuz 2200 obviously led a hard life working in the Turkish construction industry. (Courtesy Rik Meeder)

BMC

Whilst the original BMC name had been dropped by Leyland in 1970, the brand continued as a major force in Turkey where the original concern had played a significant role in the development of the Turkish automotive industry.

Whilst the first light commercial vehicle series badged as Leyland was introduced in 1980, it was the Leyland G-cabbed Yavuz series trucks introduced in 1984 that helped BMC dominate the domestic market. These were followed up with the Fatih series trucks, equipped with Cummins engines in accordance with the licence agreement signed in 1986. Following the licence agreement, which helped establish BMC as a major truck builder, all shares of the company were acquired by Çukurova Holding, one of the leading conglomerates in Turkey.

DAC

DAC trucks were produced by Autocamioane Brasov, the same Romanian company that manufactured Roman trucks. The company was established after WWII on the foundation of the old ROMLOC automotive factory, originally built in 1921. During the 1970s DAC used the same platform as ROMAN trucks, but was not part of the joint venture between Roman and MAN.

In 1976, DAC introduced a 360bhp V8, produced in conjunction with the Austrian company AVL, and in 1989 the company switched to Caterpillar diesels.

DAF

The 1980s heralded the introduction of the second generation 2800 series, and also a new bonneted version dubbed the N2800. This was a new 6x4 chassis, designed to replace the DAF-engined International

DAC was a major force in Romania during the 1980s. (Courtesy George B)

Paystar, which had been foisted on DAF when International Harvester had previously acquired a 33 per cent stake in the Dutch truck manufacturer. The N-series was primarily designed as an on/off road tipper for Middle Eastern and African export markets.

DAF had entered the 1980s in high spirits, but behind the scenes its partnership with International Harvester was not going smoothly. Whilst the company had enjoyed the financial support of IH, the deal had never brought about any design, technology or market-sharing benefits, and poor exchange rates between the

DAF had a second generation 2800 series for the 1980s. This 6x4 version, rated at 120 GTW, is still working three decades later. (Courtesy Mike Glendinning)

The bonneted N2800 was introduced to replace the ill-fated Paystar. It was aimed primarily at export markets. (Courtesy Niels Jansen)

US and Europe had effectively killed off any hopes of DAFs being sold in the US. In addition, with IH already having bought into rival truckmakers Seddon-Atkinson and Enasa (Pegaso) in Spain, its resources were spread very thin, and it pulled out of DAF in 1983.

That same year, 1983, DAF introduced the 3300 series, powered by a 330bhp version of the 1160 engine, and this became a premium alternative to the volume-selling 2800 model. This was followed by upgrades to the smaller trucks and tractors, including second generation F2300 and F2500 models featuring an 8.25-litre 250hp engine.

By the mid '80s the top-of-the-line F2800/3300 series was looking dated, but with no replacement due until the end of the decade it was given a new lease of life with the introduction of the 375bhp F3600, badged as ATI – Advanced Turbo Intercooling. The truck market loved it, and sales picked up again.

Ctn'd page 40

When Leyland merged with DAF in 1987 the resulting 95 series was badged as Leyland DAF in the UK and just DAF elsewhere.

The F2500 8x4 was initially designed for the UK market, but was so successful that DAF launched it in Holland, too. This example sports 300hp! (Courtesy Rik Meeder)

The F3600 was introduced in 1985 with engine options up to 375hp featuring advanced turbo intercooling – hence the ATI badge. (Courtesy Andrea Dal Porto)

Cab-forward DAF F2100s, such as this refuse truck, were often converted by creative dealers or specialist engineering firms. (Courtesy Rik Meeder)

Early in 1986 DAF started an intensive co-operation programme with British Leyland, resulting in DAF 8.25-litre diesels being installed in Leyland Constructors, and as the two companies worked closer together it was only natural that, following Leyland's financial woes, the two companies were merged a year later.

Whilst DAFs sold in Europe continued with a single brand name, trucks for the UK market were badged as Leyland-DAF for the next decade. One of the first fruits of the new enlarged product range was the 95 series, launched in 1987 with power outputs of 306, 352 or 383bhp, depending on specification.

Ebro

Motor Iberica was set up in Spain in 1954 to build British-designed Ford trucks under licence. The first trucks built were versions of the Ford Thames, and so were named Ebro, after a Spanish river. By the 1970s they were using Perkins engines and a Spanish version of the D-series tilt cab in light and medium weight trucks up to 27 tonnes GVW.

In 1979 Nissan Motors took a stake in Motor Iberica, and a year later Ebro launched the 'E'-Series trucks range, comprising some six models from 3500 to 11,200kg gross, and the 'P'-Series for gross weights of 13,000 to 27,000kg.

In 1987 Nissan took complete control, and from then on the company was named Nissan Motor Iberica and the trucks were re-badged accordingly.

FAP

Fabrika Automobila Priboj (FAP) is a Serbian manufacturer of trucks and buses. Founded in 1953, the company enjoys a long-standing relationship with Mercedes-Benz, which provides engines and licenses for many of FAP's vehicles. The company currently produces a wide range of trucks based loosely around components from the Mercedes-Benz 'new generation' trucks, introduced in 1974 with the SK series cab.

Following a long-standing relationship with Mercedes Benz, FAP introduced a range of trucks built loosely around the SK series that was originally launched in 1974.

Ebro launched a number of new trucks in the 1980s after Nissan took a stake in the Spanish firm. (Courtesy Richard Stanier)

Faun

Bavarian truck maker Faun GmbH had built an enviable track record as a manufacturer of all-wheel drive dump trucks, foundry vehicles and crane carriers, as well as some truly awesome heavy haulage tractors.

By the 1980s it had established itself as a leading builder of street cleaning, refuse collection, airport fire-fighting vehicles, heavy-duty tractors, and crane carriers, and its 1983 takeover of KUKA Umwelttechnik, Ausburg, made Faun the largest manufacturer of municipal vehicles in Europe. However, its range of monstrous Deutz-powered, multi-axle heavy haulage tractors are the trucks that left the most lasting impression.

With the demise of Scammell, German-built Faun became the tractor of choice for British heavy haulage firms. (Courtesy Dave Gibson)

Triple-heading Faun 8x8s in South Africa make a truly awe-inspiring sight. (Courtesy Dennis Childs)

FTF

Floor's Handel en Industrie, better known as FTF, started life as a Dutch haulage company which moved into the production of trailers in the 1950s.

By the 1980s FTF had established itself as the leading independent truck builder in Holland, specialising in heavy haulage trucks. The company avoided using any home-grown components, and instead sourced cabs from Motor Panels in the UK; engines from Detroit Diesel; transmissions from either Fuller or Alison, and axles from Rockwell or Kirkstall.

During the 1980s FTF used the same Motor Panels cab as Foden. This 8x4 version was powered by a 550hp Detroit Diesel 8V92TA. (Courtesy Rik Meeder)

GINAF

Dutch specialist truck builder GINAF started refurbishing US ex-army REO 6x6s into dump trucks in the 1960s, and managed to carve out a healthy niche market. It installed DAF diesels, and as sales increased, became certified as a truck builder in its own right using DAF axles and coachbuilt cabs.

As sales boomed, however, it started using DAF cabs, and because of this GINAF trucks often looked like modified DAFs. But underneath, the custom-built chassis and running gear were all sourced by GINAF, often using refurbished REO components. In 1980 the first of the F480 8x8s were produced: these were the very first GINAFs built entirely from new components. Two years later, a contract with DAF was agreed for the sales and service of GINAF products.

During the 1980s GINAF developed trucks with increasingly higher payloads: the advent of new heavier components made possible massive five axle 50 tonne GVW 10x8s, and in 1986 GINAF introduced its unique hydraulic suspension system. Two years later the company introduced its modular construction method, whereby it builds trucks in modules, allowing greater flexibility and diversity of models.

The GINAF F480 8x8 was introduced in 1980. Designed originally as a dump truck, this version was later modified as a heavy haulage tractor. (Courtesy Rik Meeder)

IPV

Mafsa started in 1965 as a joint venture of three local automotive workshops which had been for many years re-conditioning ex-Spanish Civil War lightweight 4x4 trucks, mostly of Italian OM manufacture, and fitting them with diesel engines. In 1972 the brand name was switched to IPV, and the model range expanded up to a 270hp 24 tonne GW 6x6.

IPV trucks were originally based on ex military vehicles, but by the 1980s the Spanish firm was building high powered all-wheel-drive trucks. (Courtesy Rik Meeder)

Iveco

Founded in Turin, Italy, in 1975, Industrial Vehicles Corporation is controlled by Fiat. The original merger of Unic from France and Magirus from Germany, with OM Lancia and Fiat commercials from Italy, witnessed a rationalisation of brands, engines, and cabs under the Iveco badge.

Following the launch of the range-topping 190 series, Iveco launched the heavyweight Turbostar series in 1984, which finally put Iveco on the map as a manufacturer in its own right. Two years later, Iveco Ford Truck Ltd was incorporated: an equal share joint venture with Ford, which took over production and sales of the major vehicles in the Iveco and Ford Cargo ranges. Under this deal, the Ford cargo was re-branded Iveco Ford Cargo and was replaced five years later by the Iveco Eurocargo.

Iveco capped off the decade with the 1989 launch of the 17-litre 480hp TurboStar V8, which it branded 'Europe's Most Powerful Truck.'

Iveco 330-42 8x4. (Courtesy Andrea Dal Porto)

Iveco 330-35 6x4. (Courtesy Andrea Dal Porto)

Jelcz

Polish truck maker Jelcz has a relatively short history compared with many of the old-established firms. Following a decision to use a former German armaments factory in Jelcz-Laskowice, near Oława, for vehicle production, a company called Zakłady Budowy Nadwozi Samochodowych (factory for building car-bodies) was established to build both Jelcz and Star trucks.

Jelcz initially used a development of the Leyland 680 engine, but by the late 1970s had switched to engines sourced from Berliet, such as the 320bhp V8.

A new cab was introduced in 1978, versions of which are still in use today on the military trucks produced by the company.

This Polish-built Jelcz 6x2 sports the new cab introduced in the late 1970s. (Courtesy Juraj Hlavac)

Kaelble

At the beginning of the 1970s, Kaelble decided to pull the plug on engine building and switch to proprietary units from the likes of Magirus Deutz or Mercedes. It focused on building a limited range of crane carriers, heavy haulage tractors, and liquid slag carriers which could cope with loads of up to 150 tonnes.

In 1979 the firm was acquired by the Libyan company Lafico, which became the principal client of the company's trucks in an ill-fated venture. Kaelble built a limited number of specialised trucks during the 1980s, including heavy haulage tractors for the German railway, Deutsche Bahn (DB), but eventually went into administration during the following decade.

Kaelble built a limited number of specialised trucks during the 1980s, including heavy haulage tractors for the German railway. (Courtesy Richard Stanier)

While Skoda continued to build trucks designed in the 1950s, LIAZ introduced more modern designs that remained in production throughout the 1980s. (Courtesy Juraj Hlavac)

LIAZ

LIAZ (LIberecké Automobilové Závody) was originally a division of Skoda, the Czech auto maker, but became independent of it in 1953, although it continued to use the Skoda LIAZ name until 1984. The 100-series was introduced in 1974 and remained in production throughout the 1980s and into the 1990s.

MAN

MAN entered the 1980s on a high after its top-of-the range 320bhp V10-powered 19.321 series was voted Truck of the Year in 1980, and its newly-launched G-series, developed in conjunction with Volkswagen, was selling well in the 6-9 tonne GVW range.

Despite its partnership with Saviem coming to an end in the late 1970s, the Nürnberg-based truck builder continued using the French manufacturer's cab design until its long haul F90 was launched in 1986. This had been in development since 1980, and was voted Truck of the Year in 1987. The F90 range came equipped with six in-line turbocharged and intercooled diesels with power outputs from 150 to 360hp, and such innovations as front disc brakes and ABS.

MAN continued to use the Saviem-designed cab well into the 1980s. (Courtesy Rik Meeder)

This 10x8 dump truck was built by a Dutch MAN dealer to take advantage of the 50 tonne GVW allowed for such combinations in the Netherlands. (Courtesy Rik Meeder)

This MAN 35-422 sports the new F90 cab introduced in 1986. (Courtesy Rik Meeder)

This 502hp MAN 8x4 was a more than adequate heavy haulage machine. (Courtesy Rik Meeder)

MAN F90 19-422 50 tonne tanker in Holland. (Courtesy Rik Meeder)

Magirus Deutz

Magirus Deutz entered the UK market in something of a whirlwind of howling air-cooled diesels in the 1970s, and took the truck market, and in particular the construction sector, by storm. Six, eight, ten and even 12-cylinder Deutz V-engines, right up to the massive 17-litre 340bhp powerhouse, were common, and the opening of a purpose-built UK administration centre gave the company an air of longevity.

However, behind the scenes its parent company was looking to unload Magirus, and eventually the company was absorbed into the Fiat-led Industrial Vehicle Corporation, Iveco. Over the next few years model and engine integration took place, and in 1976 the first bonneted Magirus trucks appeared with water-cooled Fiat diesels instead of the traditional howling Deutz air-cooled diesel. The Magirus cabs were phased out and replaced by standard Iveco Fiat items.

Despite becoming part of the Iveco conglomerate in 1975, the Magirus brand, complete with howling air-cooled Deutz diesels, was still going strong in the 1980s. (Courtesy Rik Meeder)

As Iveco developed as both a brand and a manufacturer, so the Magirus brand was sidelined, and the famous 'Spire' insignia was removed from the grille. Sadly, time was up for the brand in 1983, when the last trucks badged as Magirus Deutz left the Ulm factory and the bonneted F range was discontinued. It is believed that some smaller trucks bearing the Magirus legend were built in Italy for export markets until the end of the decade.

Although it looks more like a Fiat, the Magirus 190.30 sports a howling Deutz diesel under the Fiat cab. (Courtesy Rik Meeder)

Traditional bonneted 'Maggies' remained in limited production during the 1980s, such as this 310hp Deutz-powered V10 machine. (Courtesy Rik Meeder)

Mercedes-Benz

The SK 'New Generation' Mercedes-Benz range, which had been introduced in 1974, formed the backbone of the heavy-duty range rolled into the 1980s. The range-topping OM403 15.95-litre V10, which produced 320bhp continued into the new decade as a popular standard fitment in place of the 12.8-litre OM402 256hp V8.

Mercedes' modular engines had been designed from the outset for turbocharging, however, and when the 14.3-litre OM422 280hp V8 was introduced in 1979 – followed a year later by the 330hp turbocharged OM422A and the 375hp OM422 LA, with both turbocharging and intercooling (the first intercooled Mercedes-Benz truck engine) – many customers

Cnt'd page 58

This Mercedes-Benz Powerliner 3033 8x4 proved a popular heavy haulage tractor across Europe. (Courtesy Rik Meeder)

6x6 dump trucks such as this 2628 were the mainstay of the European construction industry in the 1980s. (Courtesy Rik Meeder)

Mercedes-Benz SK 320hp V10 Powerliner 8x4. (Courtesy Rik Meeder)

This V10-powered 2033 6x2 was operated by Shell in Holland at the legal maximum GTW of 50 tonnes, and could carry 48,000 litres of petrol. (Courtesy Rik Meeder)

remained sceptical about this 'new' technology, and opted for naturally aspirated engines.

However, even the sceptics were eventually won over, and by 1985 the naturally aspirated V10, having had its cubic capacity increased to 18.3, was mainly only used in construction trucks. For special application there was even a turbocharged and intercooled V10 with a beefy 500bhp V12 available for special applications.

MOL

The Belgian MOL company was first formed in 1952 and started out re-building and modifying surplus military

Mercedes-Benz SK 2033 6x2 operating at 50 tonnes GTW in Holland. (Courtesy Rik Meeder)

trucks left behind in Europe after WWII. It built trucks under its own name from 1966 onwards, specialising in on-off road, construction, oilfield, and heavy haulage tractors. The company mostly used Magirus-Deutz air-cooled diesels, although Cummins and GM engines became later options.

ÖAF

ÖAF are the initials of Österreichische Automobil-Fabrik, an Austrian truck builder which merged with Gräf & Stift and then became a wholly-owned subsidiary of MAN in 1971.

Since the 1970s, ÖAF had specialised in building municipal trucks, such as refuse collection vehicles and

MAN's Austrian specialist truck division, ÖAF, entered the 1980s using the old Saviem-designed cab such as this one here on this chunky 40-331 6x6 operating in Russia. (Courtesy Max Chern)

ÖAF adopted the new F90 cab in 1986, as seen here on this 500hp 8x8. (Courtesy Len Rogers)

specialist multi-axle heavyweights which are usually badged as MAN.

Pegaso

The 1980s were tough times for Enasa, the Spanish parent company of Pegaso trucks. The European truck market had become so competitive and saturated that Enasa sought joint ventures with other truck makers to help reduce its development costs.

In 1983 it acquired Seddon-Atkinson from International Harvester, making it a division of Enasa, and then followed up with a joint venture with DAF under which it produced the new cab for the DAF 95 series, as well as for the Pegaso Troner and the Seddon-Atkinson Strato.

Ctn'd page 65

'Chinese Six' twin-steer trucks, such as this Pegaso Tecno, continued being popular in Spain well into the 1980s. (Courtesy Rik Meeder)

Ending its days in Chile: a Pegaso Tecno 8x4. (Courtesy Javier)

Pegaso Troner 360 8x2. (Courtesy Rik Meeder)

Holland was one of the few countries where Pegasos were sold outside of their native Spain. (Courtesy Rik Meeder)

Enasa was in turn acquired by Iveco in 1990, and most of the Pegaso products were discontinued shortly afterwards.

Praga

As the name implies, Praga is a truck manufacturer based in Prague, in the Czech Republic.

The Praga V3S 6x6 range was introduced in 1952, primarily as a go-anywhere vehicle, and remained in production right through the 1980s. It was powered by a 7.4-litre air-cooled in-line six, based on half of a Tatra V12 diesel from the T111. It was supplemented by the 5ST 4x2 which was aimed more at the civilian market.

The Praga V3S 6x6 had its roots in the 1950s, but was still in production in the 1980s. (Courtesy Juraj Hlavac)

RABA

The Hungarian Railway Carriage and Machines Works in Gyor had built RABA branded trucks under licence from both Krupp and MAN prior to WWII. After the cessation of hostilities in Europe, the Soviets hived off many of the former RABA products to other Eastern Bloc plants, leaving Gyor to produce just axles, steering gear, and transmissions.

However, following the purchase of a new engine

RABA ditched the Saviem-MAN cab in the 1970s and switched to the DAF cab, which remained in production throughout the 1980s.

manufacturing licence from MAN in 1967, RABA quickly got back into truck manufacturing. After building a prototype with a British-built Motor Panels cab, RABA exploited its licence with MAN and launched its first truck range in 1971 using RABA-MAN 215 and 230bhp diesels and fitted with the Saviem cab. Designed to operate at gross weights of up to 38 tonnes, they were hardly high tech machines.

This RABA F26 operated in Russia had an identity crisis. Despite having a MAN diesel, the cab proudly displays both RABA and DAF logos. (Courtesy Max Chern)

Following the launch of the DAF2800 series in 1974, RABA did a deal with the Dutch truck maker for the supply of cabs, and these improved turbocharged models were produced into the 1980s.

Renault

In 1978, Berliet and Saviem merged to form the only HGV manufacturer in France, which became Renault Véhicules Industriels; the truck division of the Renault

This Renault double trailer outfit in New Zealand would be allowed to operate at gross weights above 35 tonnes GTW. (Courtesy Trevor Jones)

Group. The Saviem brand was discontinued in 1980 along with Berliet, however the Berliet truck was continued under the Renault logo, and was further developed and exported extensively, remaining in production as the R series until 1996.

The Renault R310 was a very competent long-haul truck. (Courtesy Lex Meeder)

The old Saviem cab was replaced on the medium- and light-heavyweights with the cab from the 'Club of Four' consortium. This G280 had a design GTW of 38 tonnes. (Courtesy Lex Meeder)

R380 demountable dumper outfit operating in Holland at 50 tonnes GTW. (Courtesy Rik Meeder)

Who said they didn't rope and sheet in Europe? (Courtesy Rik Meeder)

A full load of concrete beams make an impressive load on this 50 tonne Renault R380. (Courtesy Rik Meeder)

ROMAN

Autocamioane ROMAN (with the DAC division) is a truck and bus manufacturer from Brasov, Romania. The company was established after WWII on the foundation of the old ROMLOC automotive factory, built in 1921.

In 1967 the company entered into a cooperation deal with MAN, which resulted in the production of badge-engineered ROMAN trucks: 135bhp medium weight and a 215bhp heavyweight, apparently with a design weight of 36 tonnes GVW.

In 1976 the Romanian's National Institute for Thermal Engines produced the new 360hp V8 engine in cooperation with the Austrian company AVL. The old Saviem-MAN cab remained in production throughout the 1980s until it was finally replaced in 1989, and Caterpillar diesel became an option.

The old Saviem-MAN cab continued in production at ROMAN well into the 1980s. (Courtesy Max Chern)

Saurer

Adolph Saurer AG was an Arbon, Switzerland-based manufacturer of trucks and buses, under both the Saurer and Berna brands. Saurer merged with FBW, another Swiss specialist truck builder, in the early 1980s to form Nutzfahrzeuggesellschaft Arbon & Wetzikon, and in 1982 NAW was consumed by the Daimler-Benz Empire.

Scania

Having set the European truck scene alight in 1969 with the launch of its 14-litre 350hp V8 – at the time the most powerful truck engine in Europe – the Scania 81, 111 and 141 range was looking a little dated as the Swedish truck maker rolled into 1980. However just one year into the new decade, Scania launched its new look 82,112, and 142 series.

Scania set a new benchmark in 1981 with the introduction of the 112 series with 285 and 305hp options.

T. ALUN JONES
SCANIA
TJA
TJA
T. ALUN JONES LTD.
Severn Farm
WELSHPOOL
01938 553098
HAULAGE &
STORAGE
142 H
V8
C535 HOB

Its long-serving six in-line turbocharged DS11 engine was now available in 285 and 305hp options, whilst the DS14 V8 was increased in power to 388hp. Scania also introduced a heavyweight 6x4 tractor for heavy haulage work rated at 152 tonnes GVW.

Left: The new 142 series had the power output of the V8 increased to 388hp. (Courtesy Clive Davis)

Whilst 8x4 versions of the big Scanias were never available in the UK, R142 'eight wheelers' were popular for container haulage of 50 tonnes GTW in Holland. (Courtesy Lex Meeder)

Skoda kept the old-style cab in production well into the 1980s. (Courtesy Juraj Hlavac)

Sisu continued to build trucks in Finland throughout the 1980s, during which time the old-style cab was replaced with a more modern version. (Courtesy Anneli Salo)

Skoda

Skoda entered the 1980s with a range of trucks that had barely changed since their introduction in the late 1950s. The original crew cab had been re-worked into a day cab, but the design and mechanical specification had not kept pace with comparable truck manufacturers.

Sisu

During the 1970s the main engine options for Sisu were Leyland, Rolls-Royce, and even Valmet, but when Sisu Auto Oy returned to state ownership in 1974 these engines were phased out in favour of Cummins diesels. By the mid 1980s the old square cabs were phased out and replaced with the new SR series and forward-control SM series.

Steyr

During the 1980s, Austrian truck builder Steyr struggled to make headway against the tide of stiff competition. Its dated angular cab didn't win it too many friends, although its range of diesels, up to the impressive 362hp V8, helped to keep sales rolling in. By the end of the decade the company was in crisis and eventually taken over by MAN, and the Steyr plant used for the manufacture of light and medium weight MAN trucks.

TAM

TAM had quickly become Yugoslavia's leading truck manufacturer. It had progressed from its original Klockner-Humboldt-Deutz engine licence in 1952, to a full mutual production plan with Magirus Deutz in 1972.

Left: This Steyr S1936 took part in an experiment that had trucks 25 metres long operating in Holland. (Courtesy Rik Meeder)

At its height, it employed more than 8000 workers: however, it suffered serious economic decline during the 1980s, and closed its doors the following decade.

This 130hp TAM was one of the last trucks built by the Yugoslavian truck maker in the 1980s. (Courtesy Juraj Hlavac)

Tatra

Czech truck builder Tatra had entered the 1980s with the T815 family of trucks – successors to the legendary T813, first introduced in the late 1960s. The T815s used the traditional Tatra concept of a rigid backbone tube with swinging half axles, giving independent suspension with amazing off-road capabilities.

All-wheel drive versions of the T815 included 4x4, 6x6, 8x8, 10x10, 12x8, and 12x12 configurations, with both liquid- and air-cooled diesel options.

Tatra T815 6x6.

This Tatra T815 6x6, complete with huge super single tyres, looks as though it would be more at home off-road than hauling a drawbar trailer on long-haul work. (Courtesy Rik Meeder)

Terberg

Terberg started out rebuilding and modifying former military trucks after WWII. Many former REO, Diamond Ts, and GMCs got the Terberg treatment in Holland, initially being re-engineered with DAF and Mercedes components.

By the 1980s however, Terberg was very much a truck manufacturer in its own right, and was exclusively using Volvo components to build a magnificent range of heavyweight multi-axle and multi-drive trucks.

The Terberg name is synonymous with building 50-tonne GVW dump trucks like this 10x8 FL3000. (Courtesy Rik Meeder)

Terberg FL1450 6x6. (Courtesy Rik Meeder)

Cement mixers don't come much bigger than this 50 tonne GVW Terberg FL2850 10x4. (Courtesy Rik Meeder)

Chunky F1850 8x4 tractor looks like something Volvo should have built. (Courtesy Rik Meeder)

Tractor units don't get much bigger than this 480hp Terberg F2950 10x6. (Courtesy Rik Meeder)

Titan 8x8 with 520hp Mercedes-Benz V12. (Courtesy Rik Meeder)

Titan

Titan Spezialfahrzeugbau GmbH is the builder of heavy duty and specialist trucks for the heavy hauling, mining, and construction industries, as well as customising trucks to operator's requirements. The company has a long and fruitful relationship with Mercedes-Benz, and during the 1970s and '80s raided the MB parts bin to build super heavyweights which it marketed under its own brand. It regularly used standard MB 6x6 dump trucks as the basis for its creations, often installing 520hp MB industrial V12 engines for some serious pulling power.

Volvo

Volvo had launched the F10 and F12 in 1977, and quickly followed up with the 16-litre 470hp F16 – which, at the time, was one of the most powerful truck engines ever produced, so it entered the 1980s with a comprehensive range of heavyweights, geared to meet the demands of an increasingly sophisticated market.

The new heavyweight trucks, in tandem with the low datum FL series, proved the most successful truck Volvo had produced throughout the 1980s until it was replaced in the following decade.

The 470hp Volvo F16 was the most powerful truck available on the market when it was launched in 1977. (Courtesy Andrea Dal Porto)

The Volvo F10 set a new benchmark in truck sales when it was launched in 1977. (Courtesy Rik Meeder)

Although bonneted trucks were not that popular on long-haul work, vehicles such as this N12 proved popular in the construction industry. (Courtesy Andrea Dal Porto)

The Volvo N12 also proved a popular choice for heavy haulage operators. (Courtesy Len Rogers)

Long before Volvo could think about building its own heavyweight 8x4s this F12 was re-engineered by Terberg of Holland into this impressive 8x4 50 tonne GTW container haulier. What a beast! (Courtesy Rik Meeder)

TRUCKMAKERS™

Colin Peck

DAF

TRUCKS since 1949

VELOCE

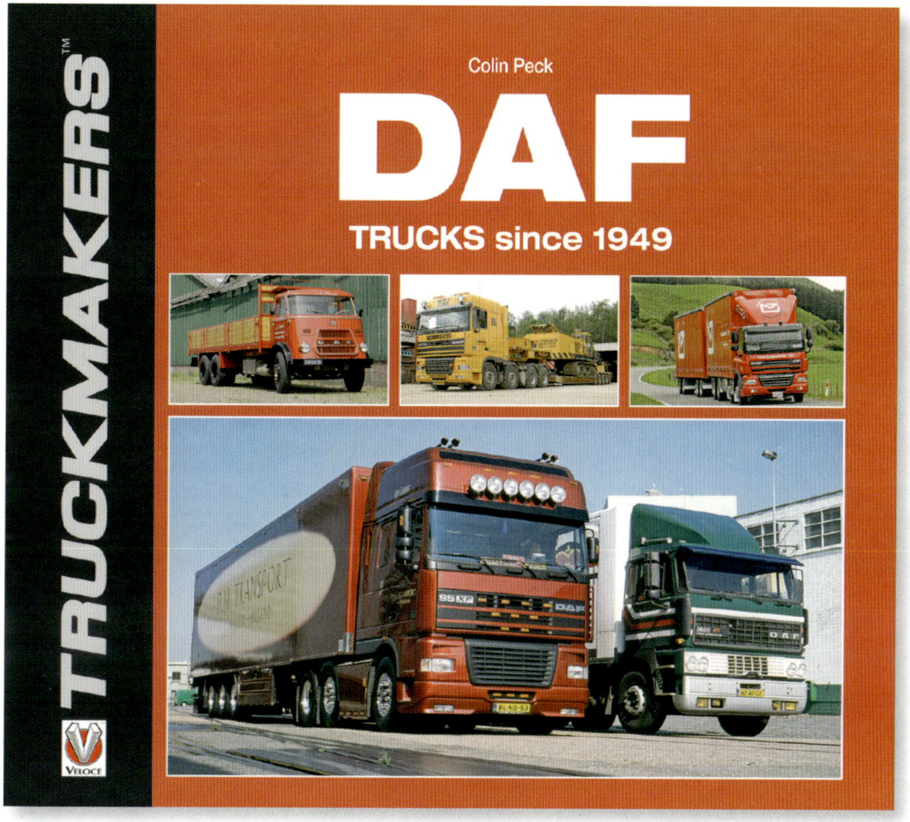

ISBN: 978-1-845842-60-4
Paperback • 19.5x21cm • £15.99* UK/$29.95* USA • 128 pages • 120 colour & b&w pictures

*prices subject to change, p&p extra

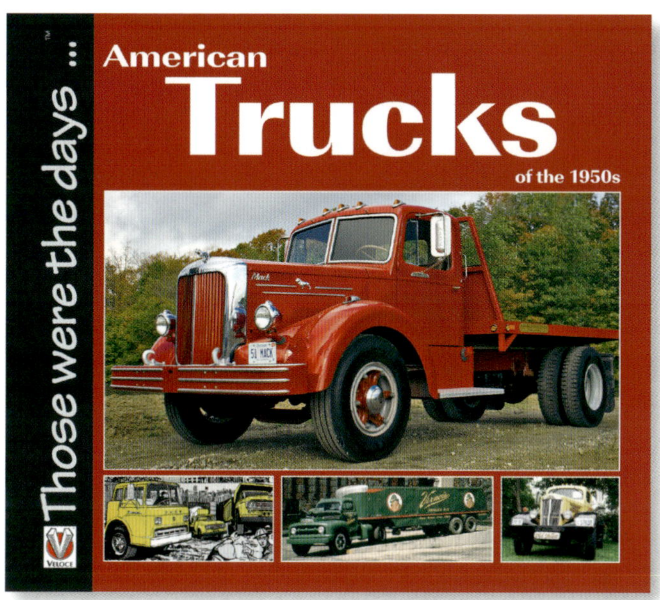

ISBN: 978-1-84584-227-7
Paperback • 19x20.5cm • £14.99* UK/$29.95* USA • 96 pages • 124 colour & b&w pictures

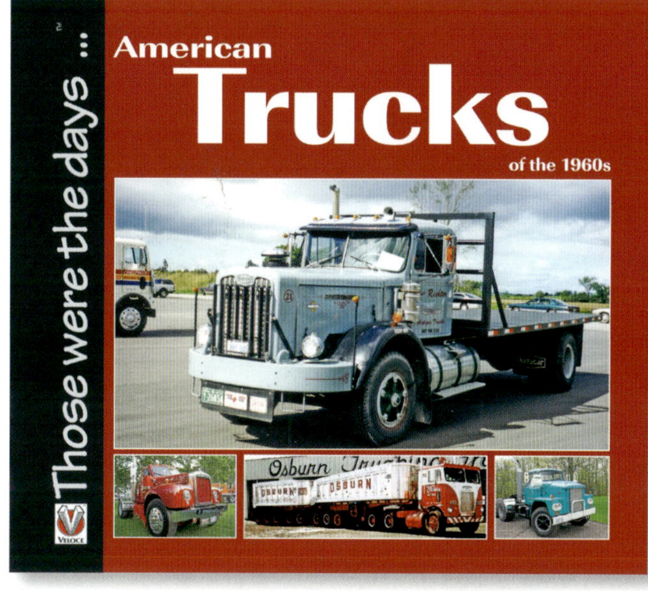

ISBN: 978-1-84584-228-4
Paperback • 19x20.5cm • £14.99* UK/$29.95* USA • 96 pages • 125 colour & b&w pictures

For more info on Veloce titles, visit our website at www.veloce.co.uk • email: info@veloce.co.uk • Tel: +44(0)1305 260068

*prices subject to change, p&p extra

ISBN: 978-1-84584-175-1
Paperback • 25x20.7cm • £7.50* UK/$29.95* USA • 96 pages • 100 colour pictures

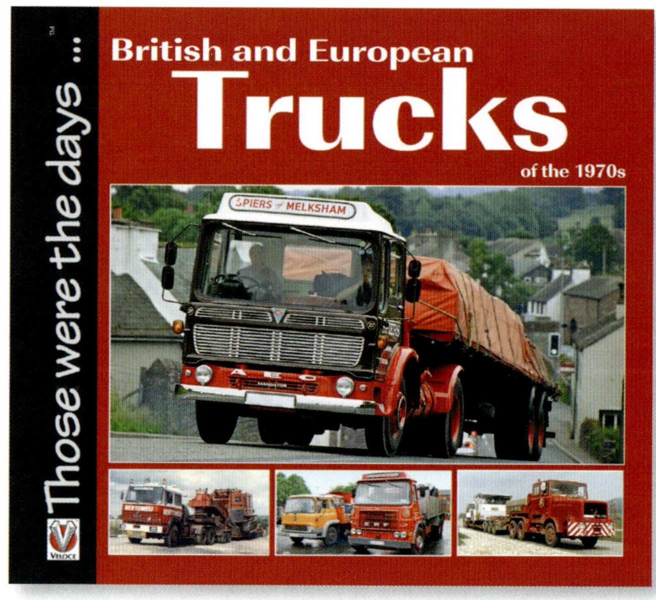

ISBN: 978-1-845844-17-2
Paperback • 19x20.5cm • £14.99* UK/$29.95* USA • 96 pages • 120 colour & b&w pictures

For more info on Veloce titles, visit our website at www.veloce.co.uk • email: info@veloce.co.uk
Tel: +44(0)1305 260068

*prices subject to change, p&p extra

Index